THE GREAT RIVER ROAD

A TRAVEL GUIDE THROUGH TEN STATES, FROM MINNESOTA TO LOUISIANA.

Copyright by Raphael marvis © 2024

All right reserved. No part of this book may be reproduced, stored, or transmitted in any form or by any means, electronic, mechanical, photographing, recording, scanning, or otherwise without prior written permission from the copyright owner.

The views and opinions expressed are solely those of the author and do not necessarily reflect the official policy or position of any other agency, organization, employer or company.

Published in 2024

CHAPTER 1: INTRODUCTION
A. The Great River Road Overview
1. Historical importance
2. significance to culture
B. The reason for the trip
1. Individual objectives
2. Anticipations

CHAPTER 2: GETTING READY FOR THE TRIP.
A. Selecting a means of transit
1. Automobile
2. motorbike
3. Cycle
4. Foot

B. Arranging lodging
1. Going camping
2. Motels and hotels
3. b&b establishments
C. Putting necessary items in your bag

1. Outfits
2. Provisions of food and water
3. Tools for navigation
4. Emergency supplies

CHAPTER 3: INVESTIGATING MINNESOTA

A. Cultural and historical background
1. American Indian ancestry
2. European colonists
3. industrial growth.

B. Natural landmarks
1. State Park Itasca
2. Superior Lake
3. Mississippi Recreation Area and National River

C. Setting out on the Great River Road trek

CHAPTER 4: PASSING THROUGH WISCONSIN

A. Cultural and historical background
1. French fur merchants
2. German emigrants
3. Agriculture sector
B. Natural landmarks
1. Apostle Islands National Park
2. Wisconsin Riverway's Lower
3. Park Perrot State
C. Traveling further along the Great River Road

CHAPTER 5: GOING THROUGH IOWA
A. Cultural and historical background
1. Expedition of Lewis and Clark
2. American Civil War
3. contemporary farming.

B. Natural landmarks
1. National Monument at Effigy Mounds
2. Hills Loess
3. State Park Waubonsie
C. Moving forward on the Great River Road

CHAPTER 6: TAKING A TRIP TO ILLINOIS.

A. Cultural and historical background
1. The first adventurers
2. The Underground Railroad
3. cities and towns.

B. Natural landmarks
1. Park at Starved Rock State
2. The Great Rivers National Scenic Byway meets here.
3. State Natural Area of Cache River
C. Moving closer to Missouri

CHAPTER 7: MAKING THE MOVE INTO MISSOURI.
A. Cultural and historical background
1. American Indian tribes
2. Influence of France and Spain
3. The literary accomplishments of Mark Twain.

B. Natural landmarks
1. The National Forest Mark Twain
2. State Park: Trail of Tears
3. Park At Onondaga Cave State

C. Driving on the Great River Road with determination.

CHAPTER 8: GETTING OVER ARKANSAS
A. Cultural and historical background
1. The Osage Nation
2. Delta area
3. History of African Americans.

B. Natural landmarks
1. Ozark Street. National Forests of Francis
2. National River in Buffalo
3. National Park of Hot Springs
C. Getting closer to Tennessee

CHAPTER 9: PASSING THROUGH TENNESSEE.
A. Cultural and historical background
1. countries of Chickasaw and Cherokee

2. legacy of music
3. Civil rights struggle in Memphis.

B. Natural landmarks
1. State Park Meeman-Shelby Forest
2. Park near Reelfoot Lake State
3. State Park Natchez Trace
C. Reaching the Mississippi border

CHAPTER 10: GETTING ABOUT IN MISSISSIPPI.

A. Cultural and historical background
1. colonial communities
2. Trade in cotton
3. Movement for Civil Rights.

B. Attractions found in nature
1. National Seashore of the Gulf Islands
2. Parkway Natchez Trace
3. Park Tishomingo State
C. The Great River Road's last section

CHAPTER 11: TAKING STOCK OF THE TRIP
A. Takeaways
B. A renewed sense of gratitude for local variety
C. Effect on individual viewpoint

CONCLUSION
A. Experience summary
B. Thank you for the chance.
C. encouragement to others to set out on like adventures.

CHAPTER 1: INTRODUCTION.

The Great River Road winds along the magnificent Mississippi River through ten states for more than 3,000 miles, from northern Minnesota to southern Louisiana. This famous route not only highlights the greatest river in America, but it also provides an intriguing look into the historical and cultural growth of the country. Starting this incredible adventure offers a multitude of activities that suit different interests, whether the goal is to learn more about American history, travel through stunning natural settings, or become fully immersed in lively local cultures.

AN OVERVIEW OF THE GREAT RIVER ROAD

1. Historical Importance.

Since the era of colonization, the Mississippi River has been instrumental in determining the course of the United States. Before European settlers arrived, indigenous peoples lived along its banks for millennia, building thriving agricultural settlements and trading stations along its rich floodplain. During the westward expansion, the river played a vital role in transportation, enabling trade and communication between far-flung areas. It continues to be a major economic engine today, supplying sectors including recreation, hydropower production, fishing, and navigation.

2. Cultural Significance

The Mississippi River is extremely significant to Americans symbolically in addition to its practical uses. Numerous writers, singers, filmmakers, and artists have been influenced by it and have tried to convey its ethereal beauty and wonder. The river and its environs served as a source of inspiration for legendary people like Mark Twain, Louis Armstrong, and Bob Dylan, who woven tales of romance, adventure, and hardship into the tapestry of American culture. Along the Great River Road, tourists will come across monuments, museums, music festivals, and creative events that serve as reminders of this vibrant cultural fabric.

THE JOURNEY'S OBJECTIVE
1. Individual Objectives.

People go on long-distance travels for a variety of reasons, such as self-exploration, strengthening relationships with loved ones, or just getting away from everyday routines. There are lots of possibilities along the Great River Road to accomplish these goals while taking in the varied scenery and interacting with the welcoming residents. Travelers can push themselves intellectually, emotionally, and physically along the route, growing in forbearance, empathy, and resilience in the process.

2. Anticipations

Adventurers have different expectations, but most have three things in common: they want to learn something new, have an unforgettable experience, and make memories that will last a lifetime. Traversing the Mississippi River's winding path offers many opportunities to realize these goals: you'll come across undiscovered treasures nestled into charming communities, breath-taking scenery unfurling from picturesque overlooks, and friendly locals ready to share tales and guidance. Above all, a positive and enlightening experience that lasts long after coming home is guaranteed when open-mindedness and flexibility are embraced.

CHAPTER 2: GETTING READY FOR THE TRIP.

Making sure your trip along the Great River Road is easy and unforgettable starts with careful planning and preparation. Timing, packing, lodging, transportation, and budgetary considerations all have a big impact on the whole trip. Travelers can concentrate on enjoying the journey and soaking in everything that the road has to offer by handling the logistics in advance.

SELECTING A FORM OF TRANSIT.
1. Automobile
Arguably, driving is the most practical way to traverse large distances and bring along the

supplies you need. Cars provide shelter from bad weather, reasonable comfort on long rides, and enough room for stuff like camping supplies or other necessities. Before driving, drivers need to consider the cost of gas, insurance, and routine maintenance. Additionally, automobiles produce greenhouse gases that exacerbate climate change. To counteract these emissions, think about funding renewable energy initiatives or buying carbon offsets.

2. motorbike
Riding the Great River Road is an exciting opportunity for motorcyclists who want to be close to nature, have wind in their hair, and take in the expansive sights. Riding, however, calls for sophisticated abilities, the right safety equipment, and alertness to any threats on the road. Before you go, make sure you are physically fit enough, know how to handle a bike, and know how to perform emergency maneuvers. Additionally, bring small, light items with you and use saddlebags or trailers to carry your belongings.

3. Cycle

Enthusiasts for cycling love the thought of cruising the Great River Road, enjoying the leisurely pace, gorgeous scenery, and sense of achievement. Riding a bicycle requires a great deal of stamina, preparation, and self-control, particularly when negotiating rough terrain or city streets. Give bicycles sturdy tyres, dependable brakes, and working lights to improve visibility. Invest in padded shorts, gloves, helmets, reflective gear, and clothes to prevent injuries and enhance comfort for lengthy rides. Carefully consider the services that are available, the need for breaks, and backup plans for transportation in case of crises while planning your routes.

4. Foot

Because of the Great River Road's immense length and inadequate infrastructure for pedestrian traffic, hiking the whole route presents considerable difficulties. However, committed walkers might tackle portions of the path, completely engrossing themselves in the surroundings and forming strong bonds with other towns. Make sure to prioritize wearing supportive footwear, packing light backpacks, choosing well-marked trails, and drinking plenty of water throughout the hike. Make reservations for motels, hostels, and campgrounds, among other neighboring amenities, after doing some research. Never withhold from someone your intended routes, estimated arrival times, and contact details in case of unforeseen circumstances.

ORGANIZING LODGING
Finding cozy, reasonably priced accommodations along the Great River Road is essential to making the trip enjoyable. There are several solutions available to suit different tastes, price ranges, and convenience levels. Consider the benefits and drawbacks of each option before deciding on a course of action based on your priorities and unique situation.

1. Going camping

While traveling, camping provides an affordable, engaging opportunity to get back in touch with nature. Along the way are numerous state parks, national forests, and private campgrounds offering accommodations for rent, including tent sites, RV hookups, cabins, and yurts. Camping offers guests access to amenities including picnic areas, barbecues, fire pits, restrooms, and showers as well as the opportunity to sleep under starry skies and wake up to the sound of birds. Know the rules about cancellations, fines, arrival and departure times, and limitations on loudness, dogs, and fires. Aside from tents and sleeping bags, don't forget to include cooking utensils, flashlights, bug repellant, and first aid supplies for your camping trip.

2. Motels and Hotels.

For weary travelers seeking refuge after a long day on the road, hotels and motels provide easy, hassle-free lodging. While independent hotels may offer distinctive character, local charm, and customized treatment, chain hotels frequently have consistent standards, loyalty points, and rewards systems. Make sure to compare pricing, go through reviews, check for availability, and make bookings well in advance. When selecting a hotel, take into account the following: the hotel's location, parking alternatives, shuttle services, Wi-Fi access, continental breakfasts, fitness centers, swimming pools, or laundry facilities. For a peaceful night's sleep, remember to bring earplugs, slippers, and toiletries.

3. Sleep-Only Hotels

Intimate, cozy settings are what bed and breakfast inns provide, which sets them apart from impersonal hotel chains. When welcoming guests, innkeepers typically go above and beyond by offering insider knowledge, pointing out hidden treasures, and serving delicious handmade breakfasts. Charming furnishings, considerate accents, and modern conveniences are common in rooms, creating a cozy, welcome atmosphere. To find trustworthy bed and breakfasts along the way, look through guidebooks, internet databases, or ask friends and relatives for recommendations. As spots fill up rapidly during busy seasons or special events, make your reservation early. Wear appropriate clothing for the multi-course dinners, strike up meaningful discussions with the hosts and other visitors, and enjoy the convivial attitude that permeates these comfortable retreats.

ESSENTIALS FOR PACKING.
Effective and comprehensive packing guarantees a worry-free, worry-free trip down the Great River Road. Bring products that are space-saving, multifunctional, and can be used for a variety of purposes. When packing baggage or loading cars, prioritize accessibility, lightweight, and efficient organization.

1. Outfits
Choose clothing composed of readily mix-and-matchable, wrinkle-resistant materials that dry quickly. Choose layers that can adapt to changing weather and temperature, such as insulating mid-layers, waterproof outer shells,

and moisture-wicking base layers. Remember to include extra socks, hats, sunglasses, scarves, gloves, and swimwear. Pick muted hues that go well with a variety of environments, and don't wear more than two pairs of shoes: cozy walking shoes and, depending on the occasion, sandals or boots. Always keep an extra set of clothes on hand in case of mishaps or unexpected changes in the weather. Separately store dirty clothes in compression sacks.

2. Provisions of Food and Water.
To sustain energy levels between meals, carry non-perishable, nutrient-dense snacks like almonds, seeds, jerky, granola bars, dried fruit, or crackers. Purchase insulated lunch boxes or portable coolers for perishables, and bring reusable water bottles or hydration bladders to refill at secure locations. Try local food and support local businesses by shopping at farmers markets, grocery stores, and roadside kiosks whenever you can. For making basic meals, cooking supplies, cutlery, and utensils come in

rather handy, and collapsible containers make cleanup and storage easier.

3. Navigational Aids.
Equip yourself with gadgets that can deliver precise instructions, up-to-date traffic information, and pertinent Points of Interest (POIs)—tablets, cellphones, or GPS units work well. Before leaving, install mapping programs, download offline maps, and cache critical files. Obtain hardcopy maps, guidebooks, or comprehensive road atlases as backups in case your technology fails. In the worst case, learn how to navigate using celestial bodies, landmarks, and compasses. Finally, become acquainted with the area codes, zip codes, and emergency numbers that are relevant to the jurisdictions you are visiting.

4. Emergency Equipment.
Stock up on the necessities for emergency preparedness: flashlights or headlamps with spare batteries; whistles, mirrors, or flares for signaling assistance; duct tape, paracord, or

bungee cords for repairs; pocket knives, multi-tools, or Leatherman devices; and fire-starting kits (matches, lighter, ferrocerium rod, or magnesium striker). All of these items are essential for handling medical emergencies. Stow extra cash, credit cards, identification papers, photocopies of important documents, and contact information for tow firms, insurance companies, and roadside help organizations.

CHAPTER 3: INVESTIGATING MINNESOTA.

Minnesota, the gateway to the Great River Road, presents an alluring fusion of historical significance, natural beauty, and cultural diversity. Explore the fascinating history and vibrant current of the state by going to important landmarks, interacting with locals, and taking part in community activities.

CULTURAL AND HISTORICAL BACKGROUND.
1. American Indian Lineage.
For centuries before to the arrival of European settlers, Minnesota was home to aboriginal tribes who established intricate communities marked by expert networks for farming, fishing, hunting,

and trading. Discover the histories, languages, spiritual beliefs, arts, and customs of the Ojibwe (Chippewa) and Dakota (Sioux) people by visiting historic archaeological sites, interpretive centers, or educational establishments. Visit powwows, rituals, or seminars organized by native groups to see live performances of traditional music, dance, storytelling, and crafts. Respect the traditions, get permission before taking pictures or recording events, and don't take away any holy items or relics.

2. Settlers from Europe.
In the latter part of the 17th century, European traders, missionaries, and explorers started making their way into what is now Minnesota, founding farms, fur trading facilities, and religious missions. The environment was permanently altered by French explorers, British soldiers, and American pioneers who built homes, churches, schools, and forts that still stand today. Explore reconstructed buildings, living history museums, or reenactments of military operations, pioneer life, or immigrant

experiences. Talk to the offspring of the pioneers, since many of them are still involved in family crafts, trades, or traditions that have been passed down through the ages.

3. Industrial Advancement.
During the 19th and 20th centuries, Minnesota's economy changed quickly, moving from agrarian subsistence to industrial dominance. Manufacturing, shipbuilding, iron ore mining, lumber harvesting, and flour milling were the main industries, drawing hordes of workers looking for work. Admire architectural wonders such as the James J. Hill House, the Mill City Museum, and the Stone Arch Bridge, which are representations of success and creativity arising from hardship and perseverance. Explore interactive displays, practical exercises, or narrated tours that highlight labor struggles, technological advancements, and entrepreneurial endeavors that influenced Minnesota's industrial landscape.

NATURAL ATTRACTIONS
1. The Northern Beaches.
Minnesota's North Shore is a rocky region that stretches about 150 miles northwest from Duluth to Canada along the shore of Lake Superior. This breathtaking area is home to immaculate beaches, striking cliffs, thick woods, roaring rivers, breathtaking waterfalls, and wildlife-rich boreal marshes. Threatened animals including wolves, moose, bald eagles, and peregrine falcons are protected by designated state parks and national forests, which maintain delicate ecosystems. Take beautiful walks, drives, or boat rides to see migratory birds, take in the expansive views, and take pictures. Depending on the season, engage in outdoor activities including dog sledding, snowshoeing, skiing, fishing, kayaking, and snowshoeing.

2. The Canoe Area Wilderness in the Boundary Waters

The Boundary Waters Canoe Area Wilderness, which spans the US-Canada border, is made up of more than a million acres of secluded, protected territory that is mostly accessible by canoe or kayak. Amidst old-growth pine, fir, spruce, and hardwood forests, traverse winding waterways that trace glacial-carved lakes, streams, and portages. Spend a night beneath the stars, go walleye, bass, or trout fishing, or just take in the eerie sounds of the local loons echoing across peaceful stretches. To protect pristine wilderness conditions for future generations, strictly follow the Leave No Trace philosophy, paying attention to quiet zones, designated campsites, and fire laws.

3. National Park Voyageurs.

Voyageurs National Park is named for the adventurous fur traders who crossed its vast network of rivers. It spans over 220,000 acres of pristine aquatic environment on both sides of the Canadian border. This vast park, which can only be reached by boat, floatplane, or snowmobile, is home to innumerable islands, bays, channels, and inlets that were created thousands of years ago by glaciers retreating. Take a personal watercraft, houseboat rental, or chartered cruise to see hidden coves, see eagles nesting, or watch otters having fun in crystal-clear waters. Participate in nighttime campfire lectures, ranger-led events, or citizen science projects tracking invasive species, signs of climate change, or wildlife populations.

4. State Park Itasca

Itasca State Park, which was established in 1891 as Minnesota's first state park, is approximately 33,000 acres of gently sloping hills, lush forests, and glistening lakes that are gathered around the legendary Mississippi River headwaters. Stroll across cobblestone shallows in your bare feet where the young river starts its 2,300-mile trip southward to the Gulf of Mexico. Stroll along woodland trails, cross suspension bridges positioned above rushing waterfalls, or ride bicycles along paved routes that connect picturesque vistas, historical monuments, and rustic homes. In the majesty of nature, lose yourself in peace, isolation, and wonder while recognizing the transient beauty of every moment.

CHAPTER 4: PASSING THROUGH WISCONSIN.

The second state on the Great River Road, Wisconsin, beckons exploration with its rich history, vibrant culture, and breathtaking scenery. There is much to explore in this Upper Midwest jewel, from its advantageous location by important rivers to its energetic cities, sleepy villages, and picturesque countryside.

CULTURAL AND HISTORICAL BACKGROUND

1. French Fur Dealers
French explorers and coureurs des bois traversed a great deal of the region long before European

settlers claimed land in what would become Wisconsin. They had profitable fur trading connections with Native American tribes during this time. Place names like Prairie du Sac, La Crosse, Green Bay, and Lac Courte Oreilles, which honor early meeting places, trading centers, or missionary stations, are testaments to their legacy. See restored forts, ancient villages, or museums that record the alliances, disputes, or diplomacy between France and the United States that shaped the dynamics of the region.

2. German Immigrants
More than four million Germans moved to the US between 1840 and 1930; many of them settled in Wisconsin to work on farms, run companies, or integrate into established communities. German culture is still heavily present in modern cheese-making, beer-brewing, sausage-making, polka music, Oktoberfest festivities, and lively Christmas markets. Visit bakeries, farmers markets, or ethnic restaurants to sample locally sourced food and enjoy classic delicacies like bratwurst, sauerkraut, pretzels,

and black forest cake. Make connections with the offspring of German pioneers and discover the hardships, victories, and legacies of their forefathers.

3. Agriculture Sector
Wisconsin's economy has always been centered on agriculture, initially concentrating on potatoes, wheat, corn, oats, barley, and animals. Later developments in irrigation, hybridization, and mechanization brought in greater diversification, efficiency, and consolidation. Wisconsin has earned the title of America's Dairyland by producing a high volume of dairy products, cranberries, ginseng, maple syrup, and organic farming. Take a tour of active farms, processing plants, or cooperatives to learn about contemporary farming methods, sustainability initiatives, or marketing tactics. Visit county fairs, cattle exhibits, or harvest festivals to celebrate rural life while indulging in handmade cheeses, ice cream, or crafted drinks.

NATURAL ATTRACTIONS
1. Apostle Islands National Park.
Apostle Islands National Lakeshore, which spans 12 miles of mainland shoreline along the South Shore of Lake Superior and consists of 21 islands, preserves a variety of ecosystems, historical sites, and amazing geological features. Hikers, birdwatchers, and beachcombers delight in natural settings teaming with flora and fauna, while kayakers, sailors, or powerboaters can explore sea caves, lighthouses, shipwrecks, or abandoned quarries. In order to camp overnight on approved island locations and witness breathtaking sunsets, glowing creatures, or displays of the Northern Lights, backpackers may reserve permits.

2. Wisconsin Riverway's Lower.

The Lower Wisconsin River meanders gently southward from Sauk City to Prairie du Chien, traversing a wide basin bordered by heavily forested bluffs, sandbars, marshes, and wetlands. This gorgeous river is well-liked for fishing, canoeing, kayaking, tubing, and viewing wildlife such as eagles, ospreys, herons, deer, muskrats, and beavers. Campsites that have been established along the bank encourage overnight stays, allowing guests to enjoy the peace and serenity of this still-largely-undeveloped area.

3. Park Perrot State
Perrot State Park is a remarkable topography with a variety of habitats and captivating views, perched on limestone bluffs above the junction of the Mississippi and Trempealeau Rivers. Follow beautiful paths that lead to Perrot Ridge, Mount Pisgah, or Brady's Bluff, stopping along the route to take in views of the surrounding valleys, ridgelines, or streams below. Descend into deep forests that are home to endangered species of plants, animals, and fossils that bear witness to the millions of years of geologic

change. Swimmers dive into cold, refreshing waters that provide a little relief from the summer heat, while anglers throw lines in search of prize fish hiding beneath calm surfaces.

TRAVELING FURTHER ALONG THE GREAT RIVER ROAD.

The Great River Road next enters Iowa, a state known for its undulating plains, abundant farmlands, and historic villages, after departing Wisconsin. Follow this fabled road to explore the best parts of Iowa's history, culture, and breathtaking natural features!

CHAPTER 5: GOING THROUGH IOWA.

The third state on the Great River Road, Iowa, offers a captivating story of cultural diversity, historical significance, and agricultural brilliance. Travelers discover modern accomplishments, remnants of the past, and friendly friendliness that come to characterize this Heartland gem.

CULTURAL AND HISTORICAL BACKGROUND.

1. Expedition of Lewis and Clark.
As the starting point for their historic westward voyage, Iowa was essential to the Lewis and Clark Expedition. Meriwether Lewis spent many

weeks at the Council Bluffs Military Post en way to St. Louis, where he gathered supplies, recruited soldiers, and plotted with military commanders. William Clark, in the meantime, engaged in interactions with Native American tribes and mapped uncharted territory while surveying the upper Missouri River. Pay respect to these courageous explorers who profoundly altered the course of American history by retracing their paths through interpretative centers, museums, or memorials strewn throughout the countryside.

2. American Civil War.
Iowa made significant contributions to the Union forces during the tumultuous American Civil War by deploying tens of thousands of soldiers, manufacturing munitions, and raising money for the cause. Within its boundaries, there were several conflicts, most famously the Battle of Athens and the Battle of Keokuk, which featured Confederate raids on federal fortifications. See conserved battlegrounds, graveyards, or historical locations honoring slain warriors,

unsung heroes, and crucial moments that shaped this sad period of American history.

3. Contemporary Farming.
These days, maize, soybeans, cattle, hogs, eggs, and dairy products bring in billions of dollars annually, and Iowa is the world's agricultural leader. Modern technology powers techniques like conservation tillage, drainage control, genetically modified crops, and precision farming, increasing yields while preserving resources. Plan visits to extension offices, research facilities, or family farms to gain an understanding of how market trends, environmental stewardship, or contemporary agricultural techniques affect rural livelihoods. Take part in cattle auctions, agricultural tours, or harvest festivals to experience the genuine flavors and companionship that define Iowan culture.

Watch this space for more on the captivating displays of Mother Nature herself that may be found along Iowa's Great River Road!

NATURAL ATTRACTIONS.

1. National Monument at Effigy Mounds
Effigy Mounds National Monument, which overlooks the Mississippi River Valley in northern Iowa, is home to more than 200 ancient mounds that were built between 500 BC and 1300 AD by Native American tribes. The many shapes that these clay constructions take on, such as bears, birds, bison, lynxes, and other creatures, are said to symbolize clan identities, cosmological ideas, or spiritual relationships to the land. Wander across hallowed grounds, reflecting on the deep knowledge ingrained in these quiet sentinels that whisper secrets of long-gone old lifeways.

2. Hills Loess.

The Loess Hills are a thin strip of wind-blown sediment that is exclusive to North America and stretches 200 miles along the western border of Missouri and Iowa. These ethereal hills, which were formed during the last Ice Age, stand out significantly from nearby lowlands in terms of topography, soil composition, and ecological traits. Climb lookouts, ride paths, or cycle loops to discover unique plant life, mysterious animal occupants that have adapted to live here, and stunning views. Interact with researchers, teachers, or volunteers who are dedicated to protecting this delicate environment for future generations.

3. State Park Waubonsie.
Waubonsie State Park, which is tucked away in the southeast of Iowa, captivates tourists with its rolling hills, lush forests, and peaceful ambiance. Numerous hiking paths wind through untamed areas, offering access to expansive views, streams that are fed by springs, or secret nooks that are home to a diverse range of plants and animals. Make camp beneath a canopy of stars,

share tales around flickering bonfires, or wake up to the sound of birds greeting the dawn. For people of all ages and skill levels, Waubonsie State Park offers unforgettable experiences, whether they are looking for quiet time, time spent in nature, or healthy enjoyment.

MOVING FORWARD ON THE GREAT RIVER ROAD.

After leaving Iowa behind, the Great River Road takes us to Illinois, a state full of natural beauties, cultural vibrancy, and historical significance. Prepare to discover the secrets hidden within this Land of Lincoln!

CHAPTER: 6 TAKING A TRIP TO ILLINOIS.

Travelers are drawn to Illinois, the fourth state on the Great River Road, by its diverse history, vibrant culture, and breathtaking scenery. Known as the "Land of Lincoln," this dynamic area entices inquisitive minds with layer after layer of engrossing tales.

CULTURAL AND HISTORICAL BACKGROUND.
1. Pioneering Explorers.
Native American tribes inhabited these regions for millennia before European settlers claimed Illinois, leaving evidence of their presence in the form of mounds, petroglyphs, or abandoned

settlement remains. Later, in 1673, French explorers Marquette and Jolliet crossed the Illinois River, and shortly after, La Salle founded Fort Crevecoeur close to modern-day Peoria. Catholic missions and trading posts sprung up as French influence increased, promoting relationships with the native tribes until British power took over in the middle of the 18th century. Discover shards of this colonial history via historical reenactments, informative centers, and scattered archeological digs around the state.

2. The Underground Railroad.
During the antebellum era, Illinois was a major player in the Underground Railroad, a clandestine system that assisted slaves in escaping to freedom. Due to its advantageous location near states that allowed slavery, abolitionists gave resources, support, and safety to runaway slaves who were frantic to be freed. See preserved stations, safe houses, or conductors' homes that serve as a monument to brave people who gave their all to protect human dignity. Honor the contributions of Frederick

Douglass, John Brown, and Harriet Tubman, whose unceasing advocacy sparked public opinion and increased the pace of emancipation.

3. Cities and Towns.
Illinois of today is home to vibrant urban centers that are teeming with people, business, and creativity. Chicago, the gem in the crown, is renowned throughout the world for its award-winning food, world-class museums, stunning architecture, and exciting entertainment options. Smaller cities with interesting sights, festivals, or athletic events to experience, including Springfield, Peoria, Rockford, or Quincy, are also worth visiting. Take in the colorful microcosms around you and interact with people from other communities, creative businesses, or forward-thinking artists who are shaping the future.

Anticipate exploring the natural charms of Illinois along the Great River Road, where

Mother Nature displays her breathtaking creations!

NATURAL ATTRACTIONS.
1. Park at Starved Rock State

Starved Rock State Park, which is about an hour's drive west of Chicago, beckons tourists to discover its spectacular beauty with its towering sandstone cliffs, deep ravines, gushing waterfalls, and lush woodlands. This cherished 2,630-acre park was created in 1911 and contains 18 canyons that were created 12,000 years ago by glacial flow. Explore clearly designated paths, climb steep staircases, or take a riverboat ride to witness breathtaking scenery, rare animal encounters, or peaceful retreats. Winter sports in the form of cross-country skiing, ice climbing, or snowshoeing offer exciting options amid the frozen tundra.

2. The Great Rivers National Scenic Byway meets here.

After the Mississippi, Missouri, and Illinois rivers meet close to Grafton, the Meeting of the Great Rivers National Scenic Byway reveals expansive views, charming vineyards, and ancient communities. This breathtaking path, which stretches 33 miles along Highway 100, offers visitors unmatched views of merging rivers, migrating birds, or shifting foliage. Make a stop at the Brussels Ferris Wheel, Elsah Village, or Pere Marquette State Park for some extra fun, local food sampling, boutique shopping, or retro charm.

3. State Natural Area of Cache River.

Cache River State Natural Area is a remnant of ancient bottomland hardwood woods and cypress swamps that dates back 7,000 years, located deep within southernmost Illinois. Its 14,820 acres are protected and home to rare plant species, a variety of fauna, and globally significant wetlands, making it a haven for birdwatchers and environment enthusiasts. Ride johnboats through dark bayous, walk lightly on boardwalks, or set up tents next to placid lakeshores while you give yourself over to the whispers of long-gone spirits who call this place home.

MOVING FORWARD TOWARD MISSOURI.

Missouri is the next stop on the Great River Road, and it welcomes you with open arms as it reveals strands of culture, historical events, and breathtakingly beautiful scenery. As we continue our adventure across America's heartland, buckle up!

CHAPTER 7: GOING INTO MISSOURI.

The fifth state on the Great River Road, Missouri, offers a diverse range of natural wonders, history, and culture. This Gateway to the West, which straddles the East-West divide, reveals layers of engrossing stories that entice investigation and contemplation.

CULTURAL AND HISTORICAL BACKGROUND.

1. American Indian Tribes.

Numerous Native American tribes, including the Illini, Osage, Missouria, Otoe, and Ioway, called Missouri home before European settlers arrived. These aboriginal groups cultivated maize, beans, and squash, hunted buffalo, and established intricate networks of commerce, social structures, and spiritual beliefs. See tribal museums, cultural centers, or powwows to discover how, in spite of centuries of marginalization, erasure, and displacement, these people have persevered and left behind enduring legacies.

2. Influence of Spanish and French.
The first Europeans to claim Missouri were Spanish conquistadors in 1541; nonetheless, there was little interaction until France seized the region in 1682. Along the Mississippi and Missouri rivers, French settlers, missionaries, and fur traders built prosperous settlements, mingling with the native tribes and converting them to Roman Catholicism. These Francophone communities, steeped in Gallic customs, maintained their unique identities until 1803,

when the Louisiana Purchase gave the United States possession. Discover traces of this rich past in the form of surnames, architectural landmarks, language borrowings, or delectable cuisine.

3. The Literary Contributions of Mark Twain.

Known by his pen name Mark Twain, Samuel Langhorne Clemens was born and reared in Hannibal, Missouri, which is located along the banks of the Mississippi River. Twain's early life served as an inspiration for classic novels such as Tom Sawyer and Huckleberry Finn, solidifying his place as the country's most celebrated comedian, satirist, and regional writer. Explore his life, writings, and legacy by going on guided tours, visiting museums, or attending the yearly festivals honoring his remarkable career and enduring literary influence.

Let's explore Missouri's natural wonders along the Great River Road next, where Mother Nature really goes all out!

NATURAL ATTRACTIONS

1. The National Forest Mark Twain.
Mark Twain National Forest, which spans more than 1.5 million acres in southern Missouri, is a huge wilderness rich in wildlife, recreational activities, and historical value. This federally controlled forest, which is split into nine districts, is home to more than 2,000 plant species, 230 bird species, 50 animals, and 70 reptiles and amphibians. It is a place that invites

exploration and learning. Experience its winding trails by hiking, biking, horseback riding, or ATVing; throw lines in glistening streams; or set up a tent beneath the starry sky to create enduring connections with the natural world.

2. State Park: Trail of Tears.
Trail of Tears State Park, which commemorates the location of the Cherokee Indians' forced relocation across the Mississippi River in 1838–1839, is a sobering reminder of the disastrous effects of US Indian removal policies. This 3,444-acre hideaway, which is located along the banks of a river, provides a serene haven for introspection, healing, and reconciliation. Walk on paths lined with trees, go fishing in clear lakes, or watch migratory birds soar overhead to honor the sacrifices made by native peoples in the face of unfathomable hardship.

3. Park At Onondaga Cave State.
Beneath the lush woodlands and rolling hills of Onondaga Cave State Park is a subterranean

splendor unmatched by anything else. Ever since its discovery in 1839, Onondaga Cave has mesmerized tourists with its breathtaking formations, transparent lakes, and vast halls that reveal the enigmatic depths of Earth. Climb into the dark, put on hard hats, and take guided tours to see the stalactites, stalagmites, draperies, flowstones, and Helictites that have been carved by millennia of pouring mineral-rich water. Once above ground, take in the clean air, towering trees, and tumbling waterfalls while feeling appreciative of life's contradictions.

GOING STRAIGHT AHEAD ON THE GREAT RIVER ROAD.

With Missouri securely behind us, we accelerate in the direction of Arkansas, the guardian of the Deep South. As we continue our journey into the heart of America, hang onto your hats!

CHAPTER 8: GETTING OVER ARKANSAS.

Travelers are drawn to Arkansas, the ninth state on the Great River Road, by its diverse history, culture, and breathtaking scenery. This dynamic region, which straddles the Midwest and Deep South, reveals layers of compelling stories that pique interest and encourage participation.

CULTURAL AND HISTORICAL BACKGROUND.

1. The Osage Nation.

The Osage Nation once controlled enormous areas that included what are now Missouri, Kansas, Oklahoma, and Arkansas. These areas were valued for their profusion of wildlife, timber, and minerals. They held onto their autonomy and sovereignty in the face of fierce pressure from European settlers, finally relinquishing territory through a series of treaties. Through cultural preservation, economic growth, and education, the Osage Nation headquarters in Pawhuska, Oklahoma, continue to honor its great past, language, and traditions.

2. Delta Area

The Arkansas Delta region, which unfurls a patchwork quilt of cotton fields, soybean farms, and hardwood woods interspersed with quaint villages and vibrant cities, comes together at the confluence of the White and Mississippi rivers.

This rich plain, historically dominated by sharecroppers and planter aristocracy, saw historic changes in labor rights, racial relations, and political representation, which served as the impetus for contemporary civil rights struggles. Talk to local academics, activists, or historians to gain insight into the intricate relationships forming this distinct socioeconomic environment.

3. History of African Americans.
From enslavement and resistance to emancipation and racial justice, Arkansas was a crucial state in the history of African Americans. Along the Underground Railroad, people seeking freedom made their way to isolated villages where black people flourished in the face of hardship, such as Davidsonville or Helena. Aspiring politicians like Blanche Kelso Bruce and Hiram Revels opposed white supremacy during Reconstruction and were elected as the first African Americans to Congress. In the meantime, President Dwight Eisenhower and Governor Orval Faubus clashed

over school desegregation at Little Rock's Central High School. Explore these life-changing experiences and consider the legacy of optimism, resiliency, and inequality.

Next, come discover the natural wonders of Arkansas with us along the Great River Road, where Mother Nature always puts on a great show!

NATURAL ATTRACTIONS

1. Ozark Street. National Forests of Francis Covering an area of more than a million acres in northwest Arkansas, the Ozark-St. A world of craggy mountains, crystal-clear streams, and deep hardwood forests surrounds visitors to the Francis National Forests. These federally protected lands, which are home to hundreds of plant and animal species, reveal hidden jewels like the Mulberry River, Whitaker Point, and Blanchard Springs Caverns, beckoning exploration and discovery. With friends and family, create treasured experiences by hiking, biking, fishing, or camping in the embrace of nature.

2. National River in Buffalo.
The Buffalo National River, which was named America's first national river in 1972, flows through the center of Arkansas, sculpting a stunning route through verdant valleys, serene lakes, and limestone bluffs. Embark on leisurely riverbank floats while rigging smallmouth bass or greenthroat darters, or ascend strenuous paths that cling to cliff faces and offer hikers expansive views. Pay great attention to the sounds of the past, when these areas were previously inhabited by European explorers, American Indian hunters, and Civil War refugees.

3. National Park of Hot Springs.

Hot Springs National Park, which is tucked away in the Ouachita Mountains, attracts people from all over the world who come to relax in its thermal springs, beautiful scenery, and rich cultural legacy. This unusual park, known as "The American Spa," has 47 natural hot springs that have been used for therapeutic purposes since ancient times. Take a dip in the old Fordyce Bathhouse, visit galleries, or scale the summit of a mountain while admiring the coexistence of man and environment.

HEADING TOWARD TENNESSEE.
Tennessee is just around the corner, brimming with musical legacies, soulful food, and breathtaking scenery, as we wave adieu to Arkansas. Fasten your seatbelts and join us as we continue traveling the Great River Road and feel the pulse of America!

CHAPTER 9: TRAVELING THROUGHOUT TENNESSEE.

Tenth on the Great River Road, Tennessee is a state rich in natural beauty, cultural diversity, and historical significance. Nestled at the confluence of the Southeast and the Midwest, this charming area touches the souls of those who come.

CULTURAL AND HISTORICAL BACKGROUND.

1. Nations of Chickasaw and Cherokee.
Tennessee used to be the ancestral home of many Native American tribes, such as the Cherokee and Chickasaw nations. These two groups established prosperous cultures that were distinguished by intricate social networks, exceptional agricultural skills, and expert craftsmanship. Sadly, these communities were devastated by Euro-American expansion and the removal procedures that followed, dispersing the survivors throughout Oklahoma, Alabama, and other states. In an effort to conserve indigenous legacy and teach visitors about their tenacity and resolve, organizations such as the Sequoyah Birthplace Museum and the Tennessee American Indian Association work to this day.

2. Musical Heritage.
From rock 'n' roll to soul, from blues to country, Tennessee's musical legacy is felt all over the

world, influencing fans and musicians for years to come. Explore the history of American music starting in Memphis, the home of rock 'n' roll, and continuing through Sun Studio, Stax Records, or the Blues Hall of Fame. To the east, the Grand Ole Opry, the Country Music Hall of Fame, and Ryman Auditorium in Nashville entice visitors, and the Women's Basketball Hall of Fame in Knoxville honors significant female coaches and players. Tennessee maintains a consistent speed, encouraging everyone to participate in on the dance, regardless of their rhythm.

3. Civil Rights Movement in Memphis.
In the history of the American civil rights movement, Memphis has played a crucial role as a battleground and a bastion for justice and equality. The city saw the killing of Martin Luther King Jr. at the Lorraine Motel, which is now the National Civil Rights Museum. This location served as ground zero for King Jr.'s final campaign. Other historical sites, such as Clayborn Temple or Mason Temple, are the sites

of peaceful demonstrations, boycotts, and talks that shocked the nation and inspired its people to face bigotry and racism head-on.

Come along with us as we explore the natural wonders of Tennessee along the Great River Road, where Mother Nature creates an environment fit for wonder and adventure!

NATURAL ATTRACTIONS.
1. State Park Meeman-Shelby Forest.
Meeman-Shelby Forest State Park protects 13,476 acres of old hardwood forests, unspoiled marshes, and rolling topography as it straddles the eastern banks of the massive Mississippi River. Travelers swarm to this lush haven because it offers peace, quiet, and connection to the natural world. Take on 20 miles of hiking trails, ride 12 miles of horse trails, or cast a line

into peaceful Wolf River Harbor in the hopes of catching a bite from a largemouth bass or a brazen blue catfish.

2. Park near Reelfoot Lake State.
Situated in the northwest region of Tennessee, Reelfoot Lake State Park is a charming area surrounded by a complex system of sloughs, flooded cypress trees, and oxbow lakes. This distinct habitat, which was formed by earthquakes in 1811–1812, is home to a variety of fauna, such as the Bald Eagle, Osprey, Wood Duck, and Alligator Snapping Turtle. Set off from one of three marinas, you'll glide through eerie trees in silence while keeping an ear out for any telltale signs of potential prey. Alternatively, explore the splendor of the wild outdoors by hiking along 10 kilometers of paths.

3. State Park Natchez Trace.
With its 48,000 acres of land on the stunning Highland Rim of Middle Tennessee, Natchez Trace State Park provides countless chances for leisure and outdoor activities. Once walked by

pioneers, European explorers, and Native Americans, this historic passage is now a playground for contemporary explorers. Take on new challenges on the more than 200 miles of hiking, biking, and horseback riding paths, or unwind in one of the eleven lakes, which are ideal for fishing, boating, and swimming. As night falls, huddle around a roaring bonfire while exchanging tales under a blanket of stars.

REACHING THE MISSISSIPPI BORDER. The Magnolia State, with its enticing possibilities for exploration and joy, looms huge on the horizon as we put Tennessee behind us. We then explore Mississippi's colorful past, dynamic present, and jaw-dropping natural wonders along the Great River Road. Let's get on with the trip!

CHAPTER 10: GETTING AROUND MISSISSIPPI.

The last state on the Great River Road, Mississippi, is rich in natural beauty, cultural diversity, and historical significance. The Deep South is a magical place that beckons investigation and introspection with its layers of compelling stories.

CULTURAL AND HISTORICAL BACKGROUND.

1. Settlements of Colonialism.

Established in 1699, Natchez is the oldest continuously inhabited settlement in Mississippi, existing for more than 20 years before New Orleans. French explorer Pierre Le Moyne d'Iberville founded Natchez at first. It was then ruled by the Spanish and then the Americans, which resulted in a diverse range of architectural designs, cultural customs, and historical sites. Sites like Biloxi, Ocean Springs, or Pascagoula, where African, European, and indigenous influences converge to convey narratives of survival, adaptation, and tenacity, are equally alluring.

2. Trade in Cotton.

By the late 1700s, Mississippi's agricultural economy was dominated by cotton, which gave rise to massive estates, mercantile dynasties, and a stratified society supported by Africans who had been sold into slavery. This profitable product was the lifeblood of port cities like Vicksburg, Greenville, and Tunica, which shipped bales downriver to New Orleans, Mobile, or Liverpool. Relics from this past age can still be seen in grand mansions, dilapidated buildings, and meticulously restored structures, offering a glimpse into the luxury and hardship that formerly characterized life on the Mississippi.

3. Movement for Civil Rights.
In the history of the American civil rights movement, Mississippi has played a pivotal role as a battleground and bulwark for justice and equality. From the horrible murder of Emmett Till in Money to the killing of Medgar Evers in Jackson, the state saw unbelievable acts of bravery, sacrifice, and violence. But in the midst of hopelessness, grassroots activists, preachers, attorneys, and regular people devoted to securing voting rights, integrating schools, and ending segregation grew optimism. These courageous pioneers are honored by landmarks like the Mississippi Civil Rights Museum and the

Tougaloo College campus, which inspire us to remember, educate ourselves, and take action.

Come along with us next as we explore the natural wonders of Mississippi along the Great River Road, where Mother Nature truly puts on a show!

NATURAL ATTRACTIONS.
1. National Seashore of the Gulf Islands.
Gulf Islands National Seashore, which spans from Florida to Mississippi and protects a chain of barrier islands and coastal peninsula, is home to a wealth of marine life, immaculate beaches, and crystal-clear waterways. For kayaking, fishing, or birdwatching, visitors swarm Davis Bayou, while aspiring naturalists, photographers,

and artists turn Horn Island into a blank canvas. Take a tour of Fort Massachusetts, a well conserved brick stronghold built during the Mexican-American War, or just enjoy the warmth of the sun while expressing your thankfulness for the boundless grace of nature.

2. Parkway Natchez Trace.
Nestled across the Old Natchez Trace, a once-used route by pioneers, European explorers, and Native Americans, Natchez Trace Parkway meanders through verdant woodlands, undulating hills, and peaceful streams. This picturesque byway, which stretches 444 miles from Natchez to Nashville, entices visitors with the prospect of exploration, excitement, and relaxation. Stop at approved rest areas, take leisurely hikes or leisurely bike rides where you may lose yourself in the splendor of nature and forget about time.

3. Park Tishomingo State.
Tishomingo State Park, nestled in the Appalachian foothills, entices tourists with its

untamed scenery, intricate forests, and crystal-clear streams. Hikers, climbers, and fisherman like this enchanted sanctuary, which captures the irrevocable influence of Native American civilization in the form of old stone walls, mounds, and artifacts scattered throughout the park. Take a plunge in Haynes Lake, have a picnic under the shade of trees, or just relax and listen to the peaceful sounds of nature while feeling comforted by her kind hug.

THE GREAT RIVER ROAD'S LAST STRETCH.
As we near the end of the Great River Road, pause to consider the amazing adventure that has brought us to this location. We've traveled through ten states, each with its own distinct history, culture, and natural beauty, from Minnesota to Louisiana. Along the journey, we have experienced joys, surprises, and hardships that have shaped our memories for eternity. Even

if our journey is coming to an end soon, the spirit of discovery and exploration endures and calls us to go on new journeys, no matter where the path takes us.

CHAPTER 11: CONSIDERING THE TRIP.

An unmatched chance to connect with America's rich heritage, varied landscapes, and resilient spirit is provided by a journey along the Great River Road. As our epic adventure comes to an end, let's take a moment to consider the lessons we've learned, our growing appreciation for regional diversity, and how it has affected our own viewpoints.

KNOWLEDGE ACQUIRED.
Tangible experiences bring history to life: By going to historical places, museums, and landmarks, we learn more about our shared past and come to appreciate that it is a living, breathing thing that affects both the present and the future rather than just a collection of dates and information.

Flexibility and patience are virtues: We learn the value of these qualities from navigating winding roads, erratic weather patterns, and sporadic setbacks. These qualities benefit us in many facets of life.

People make the trip unforgettable: We can develop empathy, compassion, and a greater understanding of the human condition by interacting with locals, learning about their lives, and developing sincere connections.

A RENEWED SENSE OF GRATITUDE FOR REGIONAL DIVERSITY.

Discovering the ten states bordering the Great River Road highlights the astounding diversity of cultures, dialects, cuisines, and customs that make up the United States of America. We learn to appreciate and cherish the distinctive tapestry that each region has spun, from the sweeping grasslands of Minnesota to the steamy bayous of Louisiana, and we realize that unity does not imply uniformity.

EFFECT ON INDIVIDUAL VIEWPOINT.

Traveling the Great River Road unquestionably leaves a lasting imprint on our minds, inspiring us to reconsider our presumptions, broaden our perspectives, and recommit to lifelong learning. After this journey, we have a clearer understanding of how interrelated we are, a fresh sense of purpose, and a deep appreciation for the opportunity to explore.

Therefore, as we near the conclusion of our virtual journey, dear reader, may you find solace in the words of Mark Twain: "Travel is fatal to prejudice, bigotry, and narrow-mindedness." May your own Great River Road adventure be just as life-changing, kindling a curiosity that burns brightly all the way through. Happy travels!

CONCLUSION.

SYNOPSIS OF EVENTS.
Traveling the Great River Road has proven to be an amazing experience, full of fascinating history, engaging local culture, and breathtaking scenery. We paid respect to the Native American heritage of the area and marveled at the grandeur

of Itasca State Park in Minnesota, where our virtual journey started. We ventured farther south and encountered the allure of Wisconsin's Door County Peninsula, the overwhelming strength of Illinois' lock system, and the vast and murky Mississippi as it carved its way through Missouri's Bootheel.

We carried on our journey into Arkansas, where we learned about the tragic history of the Trail of Tears and experienced the resilience of the Ozark Plateaus. When we got to Tennessee, we enjoyed the melodies of Beale Street in Memphis, thought about the seriousness of the National Civil Rights Museum, and took in the energy of Nashville's live music industry. We finally arrived in the friendly bayous and gracious hospitality of Louisiana, capping our journey in the energetic center of New Orleans.

APPRECIATION FOR THE CHANCE. Without the unwavering commitment of innumerable historians, preservationists, and enthusiastic people who have worked diligently to preserve and promote the rich heritage of the Great River Road, this journey would not have been possible. We sincerely thank everyone who has welcomed us, given their experiences, and taught us along the journey.

URGING OTHERS TO SET OUT ON ANALOGOUS ADVENTURES.

Our goal is that this examination of the Great River Road will inspire readers to set out on their own travels, discovering the lesser-known regions of our enormous continent and interacting with the many cultures that call it home. Firsthand experience is invaluable, and the excitement of making new discoveries is heightened when shared with friends, family, or like-minded others. Therefore, gather your belongings, load up, and head out on the open road; the opportunities are genuinely limitless. Happy travels!

Made in the USA
Monee, IL
18 June 2024